AI Financial Planning & Wealth Protection

How AI Coordinates Taxes, Retirement & Assets

By Joe Correa

Published by Live Stronger Faster

This book is for educational and informational purposes only. The author and publisher are not engaged in rendering legal, financial, tax, or other professional advice. Readers should consult a qualified professional before making any financial decisions.

First Edition

Table of Contents

Introduction

Most people believe taxes are something you deal with once a year. You gather receipts, submit forms, hope you did everything right, and wait to see how much money you owe or get back. Wealthy people, however, know something very different. For them, taxes are not an annual event. Taxes are a year-round strategy that shapes every decision about income, investments, retirement, and legacy. Artificial intelligence is now bringing this level of strategic financial planning to ordinary people. Instead of reacting to tax problems after they happen, AI allows individuals to forecast, optimize, and protect their wealth in advance by continuously coordinating taxes with every part of their financial life.

For decades, financial planning and tax planning were separated into different silos. One advisor helped you invest, another prepared your taxes, and a third might help with estate planning or insurance. Each professional worked with partial information, outdated data, and delayed reports. This fragmentation caused enormous financial leakage. People overpaid taxes, made poor investment decisions, withdrew retirement funds inefficiently, and missed opportunities to protect assets. AI changes this by unifying everything. When artificial intelligence connects income streams, tax rules, investment accounts, retirement plans, and asset ownership into one live system, it becomes possible to manage wealth holistically, continuously, and with precision that humans cannot achieve alone.

AI financial planning does not replace financial intelligence. It amplifies it. At every moment, AI can calculate the tax impact of earning more money, selling an investment, contributing to a retirement account, buying property, or passing assets to heirs. Instead of guessing or relying on generic advice, individuals can see how each decision changes their long-term wealth trajectory. This means tax efficiency is no longer just about deductions. It becomes about designing your entire financial life to minimize taxes legally, maximize compounding, and protect assets from unnecessary erosion.

One of the greatest dangers to wealth is not market crashes or bad investments. It is uncoordinated financial decisions. A person might invest well but withdraw money from the wrong account at the wrong time, triggering huge tax bills. They might save aggressively but miss opportunities to use tax-advantaged accounts. They might build assets but fail to protect them from lawsuits, creditors, or estate taxes. AI financial planning systems are designed to eliminate this chaos. They track everything in real time and continuously recommend the best sequence of actions to preserve wealth.

Wealth protection is not just about having money. It is about keeping it. Taxes, inflation, healthcare costs, lawsuits, and poor planning can destroy fortunes faster than any bad trade. Artificial intelligence allows financial systems to run millions of simulations that model risk across your entire financial life. These systems can evaluate what happens if tax laws change, markets shift, or your income grows. They can suggest insurance strategies, asset allocation adjustments, and trust structures that protect your wealth under multiple future scenarios. Instead of reacting to problems, AI prepares for them.

Retirement planning has historically been one of the most confusing areas of finance. People contribute to multiple accounts with different tax treatments, such as traditional IRAs, Roth IRAs, 401(k)s, and taxable brokerage accounts. The order in which money is withdrawn during retirement can dramatically change how much tax is paid over a lifetime. AI systems excel at this complexity. They can calculate the optimal contribution, conversion, and withdrawal strategy across decades. This ensures you do not outlive your money or give too much of it to the IRS.

Estate planning also becomes more powerful with artificial intelligence. Many families fail to structure their assets in a way that minimizes estate taxes and protects heirs. AI tools can model how assets will transfer, how much tax will be owed, and how different structures like trusts, gifting strategies, and beneficiary designations affect long-term outcomes. This allows families to preserve wealth across generations rather than lose it through poor planning.

One of the most transformative aspects of AI financial planning is its ability to personalize strategy. Traditional financial advice is based on averages. AI is based on you. It looks at your income, spending, investments, family structure, goals, and risk tolerance. It then builds a financial roadmap that adapts in real time. If you earn more, invest differently, or experience life changes, the system updates instantly. This ensures that tax optimization and wealth protection evolve with your life rather than lag behind it.

In this book, you will learn how artificial intelligence integrates tax planning, investment management, retirement strategies, and asset protection into a single intelligent system. You will see how AI models future scenarios, identifies hidden risks, and uncovers opportunities that most people never see. You will understand how this technology allows ordinary individuals to use the same level of financial optimization that was once reserved for ultra-wealthy families and corporate finance departments. AI financial planning does not make you rich overnight. What it does is remove the inefficiencies, mistakes, and blind spots that slowly drain wealth over a lifetime. It ensures that every dollar you earn works harder, stays protected, and grows more efficiently. When taxes, investments, retirement, and estate planning all work together under the guidance of artificial intelligence, your financial future becomes clearer, stronger, and far more secure.

This book will show you how to use AI not just to save on taxes this year, but to design a lifetime of intelligent wealth management. You will discover how to think like a financial strategist, act like a tax optimizer, and protect your assets like a professional wealth manager. The result is not just more money, but more control, confidence, and freedom over your financial destiny.

As you move forward, remember this truth: wealth is not built by chance. It is built by systems. Artificial intelligence is the most powerful financial system ever created for individuals. By learning how to use it, you gain the ability to coordinate every part of your financial life with precision, foresight, and resilience. This is the future of wealth protection, and it is now available to you.

Chapter 1

How AI Creates a Complete Financial Brain

Financial success has always depended on one thing above all others: coordination. Most people do not fail because they earn too little, but because their money is scattered across disconnected systems that do not communicate with one another. Income flows into checking accounts, investments sit in brokerage accounts, retirement funds grow in isolation, and taxes are handled separately at the end of the year. Artificial intelligence changes this by creating a single financial brain that connects every part of your financial life into one continuously learning system. This is the foundation of AI-powered wealth protection.

At the center of AI financial planning is data. Every paycheck, credit card transaction, investment trade, mortgage payment, tax rule, and retirement contribution becomes part of a living financial map. Unlike spreadsheets or traditional budgeting apps, AI does not just record this information, it understands it. It recognizes patterns in how you earn, how you spend, how you invest, and how taxes affect every move. From this understanding, it builds a dynamic model of your financial life that updates in real time.

This financial brain does something humans cannot do efficiently: it calculates the downstream effects of every decision. When you earn an extra thousand dollars, the AI instantly knows how much of that will go to federal tax, state tax, Social Security, Medicare, and how it affects your tax bracket. When you invest, it knows how that asset will be taxed if you sell it in one year versus five years. When you contribute to retirement, it knows whether you should use pre-tax, Roth, or taxable accounts based on your lifetime tax outlook. These calculations happen continuously in the background, creating a living optimization engine for your wealth.

One of the most powerful advantages of AI financial planning is foresight. Traditional financial tools show you what happened. AI shows you what will happen. It projects income growth, market returns, inflation, tax law changes, and life events into the future. This allows it to tell you not just what your net worth is today, but what it will be in five, ten, or thirty years if you continue on your current path. More importantly, it shows you how small changes today can lead to massive differences in long-term wealth.

Wealth protection begins with understanding risk. AI evaluates risk across all dimensions of your financial life. It looks at investment volatility, job stability, debt levels, insurance coverage, legal exposure, and tax concentration. For example, if too much of your income comes from one source, AI will identify that as a risk. If too much of your wealth is in taxable accounts, it will highlight future tax exposure. This allows you to rebalance your life just as you would rebalance a portfolio.

The coordination between taxes and investing is one of the biggest sources of hidden wealth. Many people choose investments based on returns without considering taxes. AI evaluates investments based on after-tax performance. A fund that earns slightly less before tax might produce far more wealth after tax. AI also determines where to place different assets, such as putting high-growth or high-income investments inside tax-advantaged accounts while placing tax-efficient assets in taxable accounts. This asset location strategy alone can add hundreds of thousands of dollars to lifetime wealth.

Retirement planning becomes far more precise when AI is involved. Instead of guessing how much you should save, AI models your future expenses, healthcare costs, inflation, and tax brackets. It then calculates exactly how much you need to save and where to save it. It also determines the optimal timing for Roth conversions, Social Security benefits, and withdrawals so that you minimize taxes and maximize lifetime income.

AI also plays a critical role in protecting assets from legal and financial threats. It monitors your exposure to lawsuits, creditor risk, and insurance gaps. It can suggest when to increase liability coverage, move assets into protected accounts, or use legal structures such as trusts or business entities. This ensures that your wealth is not only growing, but also shielded from events that could wipe it out.

The financial brain created by AI never sleeps. It watches markets, tax law updates, spending patterns, and income changes constantly. When something shifts, it adapts your strategy automatically. This means your financial plan is never outdated. It evolves with your life, keeping you continuously optimized for growth, safety, and tax efficiency.

In the modern world, complexity is the enemy of wealth. AI transforms complexity into clarity. By integrating every financial variable into one intelligent system, it gives you the power to make decisions with confidence, precision, and foresight. This is not just better financial planning. It is a new way of thinking about money, where every move you make is supported by a financial brain that is always working in your favor.

The Day Michael Turned His Money Into a Machine

Michael had always thought he was doing everything right. He worked hard, invested in his 401(k), owned a rental property, and saved what he could. Yet somehow, every year felt the same. Taxes took a large bite, his investments grew slowly, and he never felt truly secure. One evening, while reviewing his finances after another disappointing tax bill, he realized something uncomfortable: his money had no strategy. It was scattered across accounts with no coordination, like a group of workers without a manager.

A friend introduced Michael to an AI financial planning system that promised to act as a central brain for his money. Skeptical but curious, he connected his accounts. Within minutes, the system produced a complete map of his financial life. It showed him something shocking: although he was saving diligently, he was losing tens of thousands of dollars over time due to poor tax placement, inefficient withdrawals, and missed planning opportunities. His money was working, but it was not working intelligently.

The AI began by reorganizing his assets. It recommended moving certain investments into tax-advantaged accounts and shifting others into taxable accounts where they would be more efficient. It also suggested a Roth conversion strategy that would reduce his lifetime tax bill by hundreds of thousands of dollars. These were not guesses. The system had modeled his future income, tax brackets, and retirement needs across decades. Over the next few months, Michael watched something remarkable happen. His net worth started growing faster, even though he had not increased his income. His tax payments dropped. His investments became more balanced. For the first time, he felt like he was no longer reacting to money problems but anticipating them. The AI showed him projections of what his wealth would look like if he followed its recommendations, and the difference was staggering.

When market volatility hit, the system adjusted his portfolio automatically to protect him from unnecessary risk. When tax laws changed, it recalculated his strategy overnight. When Michael considered buying another rental property, the AI showed him exactly how it would affect his taxes, cash flow, and long-term wealth. Every decision was now backed by data, not guesswork.

Years later, Michael retired earlier than he ever expected. His income was stable, his taxes were low, and his assets were protected. Looking back, he realized that the biggest change was not how much he earned, but how intelligently his money had been managed. He had turned his finances into a machine that worked for him around the clock.

Michael often thought about that night when he first connected his accounts. It was the moment his money stopped being random and started being strategic. With AI guiding every move, his wealth was no longer fragile. It was engineered for growth, protection, and peace of mind.

Chapter 2

How AI Designs a Tax-Efficient Wealth Strategy

Wealth is not defined by how much money you make, but by how much you keep and how long it lasts. Most people spend their lives chasing higher income without realizing that taxes silently erode more wealth than almost any other factor. Artificial intelligence changes this dynamic by turning tax efficiency into a continuously optimized strategy rather than a once-a-year event. AI does not merely calculate what you owe. It designs your entire financial life around minimizing taxes legally and intelligently across decades.

At the core of AI tax-efficient wealth design is predictive modeling. Instead of looking only at last year's income, AI projects your future earnings, investment growth, retirement income, and tax brackets. This allows it to determine whether you will likely be in a higher or lower tax bracket later in life. With this information, it decides when income should be taxed now, when it should be deferred, and when it should be converted into tax-free growth. These decisions have enormous long-term consequences that humans almost always get wrong. One of the most powerful tools in AI-driven tax planning is account optimization. People commonly save in whatever account their employer offers or whatever their bank recommends. AI evaluates every dollar based on its tax future. It determines how much should go into pre-tax retirement accounts, how much into Roth accounts, and how much into taxable investments. It balances current tax savings against future tax freedom, creating a strategy that maximizes lifetime after-tax wealth.

AI also manages timing, which is one of the most overlooked aspects of tax planning. When you earn money, when you realize investment gains, and when you take deductions all affect how much tax you pay. AI identifies the best moments to sell assets, realize income, harvest losses, or accelerate deductions. It can delay a sale to avoid a higher tax rate or accelerate it to lock in favorable treatment. Over time, these timing decisions compound into enormous savings.

Investment strategy becomes far more powerful when taxes are included in the calculation. AI evaluates investments based on after-tax returns, not just headline performance. It understands how dividends, interest, and capital gains are taxed. It selects investments that generate more wealth after taxes, even if their pre-tax returns appear lower. It also determines where each investment should live, placing tax-inefficient assets in protected accounts and tax-efficient assets in taxable ones. Retirement planning is where tax efficiency truly shows its power. AI calculates the optimal sequence for withdrawing money from different accounts. It knows when to take income from taxable accounts, when to tap retirement funds, and when to use tax-free Roth accounts. It also coordinates these withdrawals with Social Security benefits to minimize lifetime taxes and maximize total income.

For high earners and investors, AI creates sophisticated strategies such as income smoothing, charitable giving optimization, and Roth conversion ladders. These techniques allow people to shift income into lower tax years, reduce taxable income through smart giving, and convert taxable retirement money into tax-free wealth at the optimal time. AI runs millions of scenarios to find the perfect balance for each individual.

The result of all this coordination is not just lower taxes this year, but a financial life designed for tax efficiency at every stage. AI transforms taxes from a penalty into a strategic variable that can be controlled, optimized, and used to build long-term wealth. Instead of hoping for refunds, individuals begin designing their financial future with intention and precision.

The Blueprint That Saved Sophia's Fortune

Sophia had built a successful career as a consultant, earning more than she ever imagined. Yet every year, her tax bill grew larger. She invested wisely, but she felt like her wealth was leaking through invisible cracks. When she learned about AI-driven tax and wealth planning, she decided to try it, not expecting much more than another financial app.

The AI surprised her immediately. It showed that her biggest problem was not her income, but how it was structured. She was paying top tax rates on money that could have been sheltered or shifted. Her investments were in the wrong accounts, and her retirement contributions were not aligned with her future tax outlook. It was as if her financial life had been built without a blueprint.

The AI created a new strategy. It moved part of her savings into Roth accounts, restructured her investments, and scheduled future Roth conversions when her income would temporarily drop. It even optimized her charitable giving so that she could support causes she loved while reducing her tax burden. Every recommendation was based on a long-term simulation of her financial future.

Within a year, Sophia's taxes dropped dramatically. But more importantly, her projected retirement wealth soared. The AI showed her that by making a few strategic changes now, she would keep hundreds of thousands of dollars that would have otherwise gone to taxes. For the first time, she felt in control. As the years passed, Sophia watched her wealth grow faster and more securely. Market swings no longer terrified her because her plan was designed to survive them. Tax changes no longer confused her because her AI adapted instantly. What once felt overwhelming had become manageable and predictable.

Sophia often shared her story with friends who were frustrated with their finances. She told them that the real secret to wealth was not earning more, but planning better. With AI guiding her financial life, she had turned complexity into clarity and transformed her money into a system that worked relentlessly for her future.

Chapter 3

How AI Protects Your Wealth From Taxes, Lawsuits, and Market Shocks

Building wealth is only half the journey. The other half, and often the more difficult one, is protecting it. History is filled with people who earned large fortunes only to lose them through taxes, lawsuits, poor planning, or financial shocks. Artificial intelligence changes this reality by acting as a permanent guardian for your financial life. It does not simply grow your money. It constantly shields it from threats that can quietly destroy everything you have worked to build.

One of the biggest dangers to wealth is tax exposure. As assets grow, so does the potential tax liability attached to them. Capital gains taxes, income taxes, estate taxes, and even property taxes can erode wealth year after year. AI systems monitor your entire financial structure and calculate how much tax risk is embedded in each asset. They can show you which accounts are tax-heavy and which are tax-efficient. From there, the system recommends asset placement, holding periods, and conversion strategies that reduce long-term tax erosion.

Legal risk is another silent threat. Lawsuits, creditor claims, and liability exposure can wipe out years of savings in a single event. AI analyzes your personal and business activities to determine where you are exposed. If you own rental properties, operate businesses, or have significant personal assets, the system evaluates whether your insurance coverage, legal structures, and asset ownership strategies are sufficient. It can recommend umbrella policies, LLC structures, or trust arrangements that create legal barriers between your wealth and potential claims.

Market volatility is also a major risk to long-term financial security. AI does not attempt to predict markets. Instead, it prepares for all possible outcomes. By modeling thousands of market scenarios, it determines how your portfolio would perform during crashes, inflation spikes, and long-term stagnation. If it identifies weaknesses, it adjusts asset allocation, diversification, and liquidity levels to ensure you can survive even extreme events without being forced to sell assets at the worst possible time.

One of the most powerful features of AI wealth protection is stress testing. The system runs simulations on your entire financial life, not just your investments. It models what would happen if you lost your job, faced a medical emergency, experienced a lawsuit, or lived longer than expected. This allows it to identify vulnerabilities before they become disasters. From there, it suggests emergency funds, insurance coverage, or structural changes that make your financial life more resilient.

AI also plays a critical role in estate and legacy protection. As wealth grows, the risk of losing it to estate taxes and poor inheritance planning increases. AI evaluates how your assets would transfer to heirs under current law. It calculates the tax cost of inheritance and identifies strategies such as trusts, gifting programs, and beneficiary structures that preserve wealth across generations. This ensures that what you build benefits your family rather than disappearing into government systems.

What makes AI so powerful in wealth protection is its ability to update constantly. Laws change. Markets shift. Your life evolves. Traditional plans become outdated quickly. AI systems adjust continuously, ensuring that your protection strategies remain aligned with your reality. When a new tax law is passed, the system recalculates your exposure. When your net worth increases, it adjusts your legal and insurance needs.

Wealth is fragile without protection. AI turns it into something durable. By monitoring taxes, legal risks, market volatility, and life events in real time, it creates a financial shield around everything you own. This is not about fear. It is about foresight. With AI guarding your financial future, you no longer have to worry about losing what you have worked so hard to create.

The Shield Around Daniel's Life

Daniel had spent twenty years building his business. He had sacrificed weekends, taken risks, and reinvested every spare dollar. By the time he turned fifty, his net worth was finally substantial. But with success came fear. One lawsuit, one bad market crash, or one tax mistake could undo everything. He realized that building wealth was no longer his biggest challenge. Protecting it was.

When Daniel connected his finances to an AI wealth protection system, it revealed risks he had never considered. His assets were exposed to lawsuits through his business. His investments were vulnerable to market downturns. His estate plan was outdated and inefficient. It was like discovering cracks in the foundation of a beautiful house.

The AI began reinforcing those weak points. It recommended legal structures to separate his business from his personal wealth. It adjusted his insurance coverage to protect against catastrophic losses. It diversified his investments in a way that reduced risk without sacrificing growth. It even suggested changes to his estate plan that would save his family enormous amounts in taxes.

Months later, when a lawsuit was filed against his company, Daniel felt something new. Calm. His AI-driven structure absorbed the shock. His personal wealth was protected. His financial plan remained intact. For the first time, he understood what real security felt like.

As the markets fluctuated, Daniel watched his portfolio remain steady. When tax laws changed, his system adapted automatically. His wealth was no longer exposed to the chaos of the world. It was shielded by a system designed to anticipate and defend.

Daniel realized that the true power of AI was not just in growing money, but in protecting it. His wealth was no longer fragile. It was fortified. And with that protection came a level of peace he had never known before.

Chapter 4

How AI Aligns Taxes, Retirement, and Lifetime Income

The ultimate purpose of financial planning is not accumulation alone, but sustainability. Money must last, adapt, and provide stability across decades of changing circumstances. Traditional retirement planning has often failed because it treats retirement as a single event rather than a long, evolving phase of life. Artificial intelligence transforms this outdated model by coordinating taxes, retirement accounts, income streams, and longevity risk into one unified lifetime income strategy. Instead of asking whether you can retire, AI asks whether your wealth can support you intelligently for the rest of your life.

The first breakthrough AI brings to retirement planning is precision. Instead of generic rules like saving a certain percentage of income or withdrawing a fixed amount per year, AI calculates your actual future needs. It models your spending patterns, healthcare costs, inflation exposure, and lifestyle goals. It understands that retirement is not static. Spending often rises early in retirement, drops later, and can increase again due to medical care. AI builds these realities into its projections, creating a plan that evolves as you age. Taxes play a central role in retirement success. Many retirees are shocked to discover that taxes do not disappear when work stops. Required minimum distributions, Social Security taxation, capital gains, and Medicare premium surcharges can dramatically reduce retirement income. AI anticipates these risks years or even decades in advance. It determines how much money should be taxed now, deferred, or converted into tax-free income so that retirement withdrawals are optimized rather than reactive.

One of the most powerful AI strategies is withdrawal sequencing. Humans often withdraw money from accounts in the wrong order, triggering unnecessary taxes. AI calculates the ideal sequence for every year of retirement, coordinating taxable accounts, tax-deferred accounts, and tax-free accounts. This sequencing is adjusted continuously as markets change, tax laws evolve, and spending needs shift. The result is higher net income and longer portfolio life.

AI also integrates Social Security optimization into the retirement equation. It models different claiming ages and shows how they affect lifetime income, taxes, and survivor benefits. Rather than relying on simple break-even analysis, AI evaluates Social Security as part of a broader system. It determines whether delaying benefits, coordinating spousal claims, or drawing from certain accounts first will maximize total after-tax income.

Longevity risk is one of the most underestimated threats to retirement security. Many people plan for an average lifespan rather than a long one. AI does not make this mistake. It models multiple longevity scenarios and ensures that income strategies can withstand a long life. It adjusts withdrawal rates, investment allocation, and risk exposure to protect against running out of money late in life.

Retirement is not the end of financial complexity. It is often the beginning of it. AI ensures that taxes, income, and assets remain coordinated even as employment income disappears. By acting as a continuous financial manager, AI transforms retirement from a period of uncertainty into one of confidence, clarity, and control.

When Elena Learned Her Money Could Outlive Her Fear

Elena had always believed retirement was something you survived rather than enjoyed. She watched her parents struggle, constantly worried about expenses, taxes, and medical bills. Even though Elena had saved diligently, the thought of retirement filled her with quiet anxiety. She feared making one wrong move and watching her savings disappear slowly, year by year, until there was nothing left but regret.

As she approached her early sixties, Elena finally admitted what she had been avoiding. She did not understand how her money would actually support her for the rest of her life. She knew how much she had saved, but not how it would turn into income. She did not know which accounts to draw from first, how taxes would affect her withdrawals, or how long her money would truly last. The uncertainty weighed on her more than any market downturn ever could.

When Elena was introduced to an AI retirement planning system, she expected another complicated dashboard filled with charts and projections. Instead, what she received felt more like a conversation about her life. The system asked about how she wanted to live, what she feared most, and what kind of future she imagined. It then began building a model of her retirement that felt deeply personal.

The AI showed Elena something she had never seen before: a year-by-year projection of her entire retirement. It showed her income sources, tax exposure, healthcare costs, and spending patterns across multiple scenarios. She could see how long her money would last if markets performed well, poorly, or somewhere in between. More importantly, she could see how her decisions today shaped her comfort decades from now.

One of the most surprising discoveries was how much taxes would matter. The AI demonstrated that if Elena withdrew money in the wrong order, she could lose hundreds of thousands of dollars to unnecessary taxes over her lifetime. It showed her how required minimum distributions would spike her taxable income later in retirement and how that would affect Medicare premiums. These were risks she had never fully understood, yet they had enormous consequences.

The system proposed a coordinated strategy. It recommended drawing from certain accounts early while delaying others. It suggested a gradual Roth conversion plan during low-income years, transforming taxable retirement funds into tax-free income for later life. It optimized her Social Security claiming strategy so that her guaranteed income would be higher and more tax-efficient. Every recommendation was tied to a clear explanation and a measurable outcome.

As Elena reviewed the plan, something unexpected happened. Her fear began to dissolve. For the first time, retirement did not feel like a cliff she was approaching blindly. It felt like a road she could see clearly, mile by mile. The AI showed her that she could not only survive retirement, but live well through it, even under conservative assumptions.

Years passed, and Elena followed the strategy. Markets rose and fell, but her income remained stable. Taxes were predictable and manageable. When healthcare costs increased, her plan adjusted automatically. When tax laws changed, her strategy adapted without panic. Retirement no longer felt fragile. It felt engineered.

One afternoon, sitting on her porch years into retirement, Elena reflected on how different her life felt compared to her parents'. She was not worried about running out of money. She was not afraid of tax surprises. Her wealth was not shrinking chaotically. It was flowing exactly as it had been designed to flow.

Elena realized that the greatest gift AI had given her was not higher returns or lower taxes alone. It was peace. Peace that came from knowing her money was working intelligently, consistently, and patiently for the rest of her life. Retirement had not taken away her security. With the right system in place, it had finally given it to her.

Chapter 5

How AI Preserves Wealth Across Generations

True wealth is not measured by how much you accumulate during your lifetime, but by how effectively that wealth continues to serve others after you are gone. Generational wealth has historically been fragile, often lost within one or two generations due to poor planning, excessive taxation, or simple misunderstanding. Artificial intelligence changes this pattern by introducing clarity, structure, and continuity into wealth transfer. AI does not merely help you build assets. It ensures that those assets survive you.

One of the greatest challenges in legacy planning is complexity. Estate laws, tax codes, beneficiary rules, and trust structures are difficult to navigate even for professionals. Most families delay these decisions or rely on outdated documents that no longer reflect their true financial situation. AI addresses this by maintaining a constantly updated view of your assets, liabilities, beneficiaries, and legal structures. It ensures that your estate plan evolves alongside your wealth and your life circumstances.

Taxes represent one of the largest threats to generational wealth. Estate taxes, capital gains taxes on inherited assets, and income taxes can dramatically reduce what heirs receive. AI models how wealth will transfer under current laws and projects future changes. It identifies opportunities for gifting, trust creation, and asset repositioning that reduce tax exposure legally and efficiently. By optimizing timing and structure, AI helps families preserve far more of what they intend to pass on.

AI also plays a crucial role in beneficiary coordination. Many families unknowingly create conflicts or inefficiencies by failing to align account beneficiaries with wills and trusts. AI detects mismatches and inconsistencies that could lead to unintended outcomes. It ensures that retirement accounts, insurance policies, investment accounts, and real estate all follow a unified legacy strategy rather than operating independently.

Beyond taxes and legal structure, AI addresses a deeper issue: continuity of understanding. Wealth often disappears because heirs do not know how to manage it. AI systems can document financial strategies, investment philosophies, and long-term goals in a way that is accessible to future generations. This creates not just financial inheritance, but intellectual inheritance.

AI can also simulate future family scenarios. It models how wealth distribution affects different heirs, how long assets might last, and how changes in family structure influence outcomes. This allows families to make informed, intentional decisions rather than reactive ones. It also helps prevent disputes by clarifying expectations and documenting intent.

Perhaps most importantly, AI brings humility into wealth planning. It removes emotion, ego, and procrastination from decisions that are often delayed because they are uncomfortable. By presenting clear data, projections, and consequences, AI encourages responsible planning that honors both the present and the future.

Generational wealth is not accidental. It is designed. AI gives families the tools to design a legacy that survives time, taxes, and misunderstanding. It transforms wealth from something temporary into something enduring.

The Letters Samuel Never Had to Write

Samuel never planned to be wealthy. He simply worked hard, saved diligently, and made careful decisions year after year. By the time he reached his late sixties, he had built a life of quiet abundance. A paid-off home, investment accounts, retirement savings, and a small business he was preparing to sell. Yet despite his success, a persistent worry followed him everywhere. He had seen too many families torn apart after a death, too much money lost through confusion and poor planning. He feared leaving behind not a legacy, but a mess.

Samuel had two children and four grandchildren. They loved him deeply, but they lived very different lives and had very different relationships with money. One child was financially disciplined, the other struggled. Samuel worried constantly about fairness, responsibility, and protection. He wanted to help, not harm. He wanted his wealth to support his family long after he was gone, not create resentment or regret.

For years, Samuel avoided the topic. Estate planning felt heavy, final, and overwhelming. But everything changed when he was introduced to an AI-driven legacy planning system. Unlike the legal documents he had glanced at and ignored, this system spoke in stories, projections, and clarity. It showed him exactly what would happen to his assets if he did nothing. The result was sobering. Taxes would consume a large portion. Accounts would transfer unevenly. Confusion would reign.

The AI did not judge. It simply showed him options. It modeled gifting strategies that would reduce estate taxes while helping his children now. It illustrated how trusts could protect assets for his grandchildren without restricting their lives. It demonstrated how aligning beneficiaries would prevent delays and disputes. Each recommendation came with clear reasoning and long-term impact. Samuel spent weeks reviewing scenarios. He saw futures where wealth evaporated and others where it endured. He watched how small changes made enormous differences decades later. The system even allowed him to leave messages and explanations for future generations, documenting why certain decisions were made. It was as if he were having conversations with people he might never meet.

As Samuel implemented the plan, something shifted inside him. The anxiety that had followed him for years began to lift. He no longer felt like his wealth was a burden waiting to explode after his death. It felt like a bridge connecting generations. His children understood the plan. His intentions were clear. There would be no guessing, no fighting, no silence.

Years later, when Samuel passed away peacefully, his family was not consumed by confusion or conflict. The system guided them gently through each step. Assets transferred smoothly. Taxes were minimized. The messages Samuel had recorded played softly, explaining his choices in his own words. His family felt guided, not abandoned.

One evening, months after everything had settled, Samuel's oldest grandchild sat quietly reviewing the family's financial dashboard. She saw not just numbers, but a story. A story of responsibility, foresight, and care. She realized that her grandfather had given her more than money. He had given her a map. Samuel never had to write long letters or deliver emotional speeches. The system preserved his voice, his values, and his intentions. His wealth did not disappear. It continued working, teaching, and protecting long after he was gone.

In that way, Samuel achieved something rare. He did not just pass on assets. He passed on wisdom.

Chapter 6

How AI Creates Financial Peace, Freedom, and Control

At the highest level, financial planning is not about numbers. It is about how you experience your life. Money affects where you live, how you work, how you age, and how you care for the people you love. Yet for many, money is a constant source of anxiety rather than security. Artificial intelligence changes this relationship by transforming finances from a source of uncertainty into a system of clarity, control, and confidence. AI does not promise perfection. It promises awareness—and awareness is the foundation of peace.

Financial stress often comes from not knowing. Not knowing whether you are saving enough, whether taxes will surprise you, whether retirement will be safe, or whether one bad event could unravel everything. AI addresses this by making the invisible visible. It shows you the full picture of your financial life at all times. It replaces vague fears with concrete data, scenarios, and plans. When uncertainty disappears, fear loses its power.

One of the most profound impacts of AI financial planning is decision confidence. Humans hesitate because they lack complete information. AI fills those gaps by modeling consequences before decisions are made. Whether you are changing careers, buying property, helping family members, or retiring early, AI can show you how each choice affects your long-term financial stability. This turns decisions from emotional gambles into informed actions.

Freedom is another outcome of intelligent financial systems. Many people earn well but feel trapped by obligations, debt, or fear of the unknown. AI reveals where freedom already exists but is hidden by poor coordination. It shows how optimizing taxes, reducing inefficiencies, and reallocating assets can unlock time and flexibility without increasing income. Freedom becomes not a dream, but a measurable outcome.

Control is the final pillar. Without control, money controls you. AI restores control by putting strategy ahead of reaction. Instead of responding to emergencies, market swings, or tax surprises, AI anticipates them. It builds buffers, creates options, and ensures that you always have choices. Control does not mean rigidity. It means adaptability with intention.

As AI systems evolve, they become less like tools and more like companions—quietly monitoring, adjusting, and guiding without demanding constant attention. Financial management fades into the background, allowing life to move to the foreground. This is the ultimate success of AI-powered wealth planning: not obsessing over money, but no longer needing to.

The Quiet Year That Changed Everything

For most of her life, Natalie believed financial stress was normal. She had grown up watching her parents worry endlessly—about bills, about taxes, about the future. Even when things were "fine," the worry never stopped. Natalie carried that same tension into adulthood. She earned well, saved consistently, and avoided major mistakes, yet money lived constantly in her mind like unfinished business.

Every decision felt heavy. A vacation came with guilt. A career opportunity brought fear. Retirement felt distant and unclear. Natalie did not lack discipline or intelligence. She lacked certainty. She lived with the quiet fear that something unseen could undo everything she had worked for.

The year Natalie turned forty-eight, something shifted. After another sleepless night running numbers in her head, she admitted what she had avoided for years: she was tired of managing money emotionally. She wanted a system—something that did not depend on her mood, memory, or energy. That was when she decided to try AI-driven financial planning. At first, it felt almost unsettling. The system asked for access to her accounts, her income history, her investments, her goals. She hesitated before clicking confirm, not because she doubted the technology, but because she feared what it might reveal. Yet once everything was connected, the anxiety she expected did not arrive. Instead, there was clarity.

The AI presented her financial life as a living story. It showed her not only where she stood, but where she was headed under multiple scenarios. It showed her strengths—areas she had managed well—and weaknesses she had never noticed. Most importantly, it showed her that she was safer than she believed, and that the risks she feared were manageable.

Over the following weeks, Natalie made small adjustments. Nothing dramatic. A shift in account allocations. A change in tax strategy. A clearer withdrawal plan for the future. Each adjustment came with explanation, impact, and reassurance. There were no guesses. Only choices.

Then something unexpected happened. Natalie stopped thinking about money all the time. Not because she was ignoring it, but because she trusted the system watching over it. Decisions became lighter. She took a long-delayed vacation without guilt. She explored a career change she had postponed for years. She slept better.

As months passed, Natalie noticed how different her days felt. Financial fear no longer hovered in the background of every thought. When markets dipped, the system explained the impact calmly. When tax season arrived, there were no surprises. When friends spoke anxiously about money, Natalie listened with empathy—but without sharing the same fear.

One evening, nearly a year after she started, Natalie sat alone in her living room reflecting on how quiet her financial life had become. No constant calculations. No emotional reactions. No lingering dread. Her finances were not perfect, but they were understood. And understanding had given her something she had never experienced before: peace.

Natalie realized that freedom was not about having unlimited money. It was about having enough clarity to live without fear. Control was not about micromanaging every dollar. It was about knowing that nothing was being ignored.

That quiet year changed everything. Not because Natalie became wealthier overnight, but because her relationship with money transformed. AI had not taken control away from her. It had given it back.

For the first time in her life, Natalie was not planning for money. She was planning her life—and money had finally learned how to follow.

Chapter 7

How AI Turns Wealth Into a Living, Adaptive System

Most people think of their finances as something static. A balance sheet. A retirement account. A set of numbers that either goes up or down. This outdated perspective is one of the biggest reasons financial plans fail. Life does not stand still, and neither should your money. Artificial intelligence introduces a new paradigm: wealth as a living system—one that adapts, learns, and evolves alongside you. Rather than relying on rigid plans that quickly become obsolete, AI transforms financial strategy into something dynamic, responsive, and resilient.

Traditional financial plans are snapshots taken at a single moment in time. They assume stable income, predictable markets, and unchanged tax laws. Reality behaves very differently. Careers change, families grow, health fluctuates, economies shift, and governments rewrite rules. AI is designed for this reality. It continuously ingests new data, recalibrates assumptions, and adjusts strategies without requiring you to start over. Your financial plan becomes a process rather than a document. At the heart of this living system is feedback. AI monitors your income, spending, investments, and tax exposure in real time. When patterns change, the system responds. If your income increases, it reassesses tax strategy. If markets become volatile, it adjusts risk exposure. If a new opportunity or threat appears, it evaluates impact across your entire financial ecosystem. This feedback loop ensures alignment between your goals and your reality at all times.

Adaptability is the defining advantage of AI-driven wealth systems. Humans struggle with complexity and change. AI thrives on it. It does not panic during downturns or become complacent during growth. It simply recalculates. This objectivity protects you from emotional decision-making—the single greatest enemy of long-term wealth. By removing fear and overconfidence from financial strategy, AI keeps your plan grounded and consistent.

Another defining feature of a living financial system is integration. AI does not treat taxes, investments, retirement, insurance, and estate planning as separate concerns. It understands that every financial decision affects multiple areas simultaneously. A change in tax law alters investment strategy. A career shift impacts retirement planning. A health event affects liquidity needs. AI coordinates all of this automatically, preventing fragmentation.

A living system also prioritizes optionality. Instead of locking you into rigid paths, AI ensures you always have choices. It builds buffers, diversifies income streams, and maintains flexibility. This means you can pivot when life demands it—without sacrificing long-term stability. Optionality is freedom expressed financially.

Ultimately, AI turns wealth into something that works quietly in the background. It does not demand constant attention or emotional energy. It adapts silently, ensuring alignment while you focus on living. This is the final evolution of financial planning: not constant optimization, but sustained harmony between money and life.

The System That Grew With Marcus

Marcus used to believe financial success meant vigilance. He checked his accounts constantly, followed market news obsessively, and recalculated his plans every time something changed. He told himself this was responsibility, but deep down he knew it was anxiety disguised as control. His finances were never at rest, and neither was his mind.

In his early forties, Marcus's life began to shift in ways he could not predict. A promotion brought higher income and higher stress. His parents aged faster than expected, requiring time and financial support. His children entered a phase of life filled with new expenses and emotional complexity. Every change forced Marcus back to the spreadsheets, trying to recalculate a future that refused to hold still.

The breaking point came during a market downturn. Marcus reacted quickly, selling assets out of fear, only to watch markets recover weeks later. The mistake cost him money, but more than that, it cost him confidence. For the first time, he admitted that reacting faster was not the same as reacting wisely.

When Marcus adopted an AI-driven financial system, he expected better calculations. What he did not expect was a different relationship with time. The system did not ask him to predict the future. It assumed the future would change. It built his finances around that assumption.

At first, Marcus resisted letting go. He still checked dashboards daily, questioned recommendations, and second-guessed decisions. But the system did not rush him. It simply continued monitoring, adjusting, and explaining. Slowly, Marcus noticed something strange. The system was responding to changes before he felt them emotionally. Income shifts triggered tax recalculations. Market volatility adjusted risk exposure. New expenses were absorbed without panic.

Years passed, and Marcus's life continued evolving. He changed careers, earning slightly less but gaining more time. His parents required greater care. His children left for college. Through it all, the system adapted seamlessly. There were no dramatic overhauls, no frantic recalculations—only quiet alignment.

One evening, Marcus realized he had not checked his accounts in weeks. Not out of neglect, but trust. His finances no longer required constant supervision. They were not static numbers waiting to surprise him. They were alive, responsive, and resilient.

As retirement approached, Marcus expected anxiety to return. Instead, the system presented him with clear paths, flexible options, and conservative projections. It showed him that retirement was not a cliff, but a gradual transition. His income adjusted. His risk exposure softened. His liquidity increased. Everything shifted naturally, like a body adapting to a new rhythm.

In retirement, Marcus experienced something he never thought possible. Financial silence. Not emptiness, but calm. Taxes were anticipated. Income flowed predictably. Markets moved, but his life did not lurch with them. His system absorbed shocks so he did not have to.

Years later, sitting with his grandchildren in a quiet backyard, Marcus reflected on what had truly changed. He had not become richer than his peers. He had become steadier. His wealth had matured alongside him, learning his rhythms, respecting his limits, and adapting to his needs.

Marcus understood then that the greatest gift AI had given him was not optimization, but continuity. His money had grown with him, not ahead of him or behind him. It had become a living system—one that evolved without fear, without drama, and without demanding his constant attention.

And in that quiet alignment between life and money, Marcus finally found what he had been chasing all along: not control, but trust.

Chapter 8

How AI Creates Clarity During Uncertainty and Crisis

No financial plan is truly tested during times of stability. It is tested during uncertainty. Economic downturns, sudden illness, job loss, family emergencies, political shifts, and unexpected opportunities all arrive without warning. Traditional financial planning struggles in these moments because it relies on assumptions that no longer hold. Artificial intelligence excels precisely where uncertainty exists. It does not depend on certainty. It is built for change.

Uncertainty creates emotional pressure. When fear enters the equation, people abandon long-term strategies in favor of short-term relief. They sell investments at the wrong time, delay necessary decisions, or freeze entirely. AI removes emotion from the equation by grounding decisions in probability, modeling, and preparation. It does not attempt to eliminate uncertainty. It makes uncertainty manageable.

One of the most powerful roles AI plays during crisis is scenario modeling. Instead of assuming one future, AI evaluates many. It shows how your finances perform if income drops, if markets fall, if taxes rise, or if expenses increase suddenly. These simulations are not predictions. They are rehearsals. When uncertainty arrives, the outcome is no longer shocking because it has already been explored.

Liquidity management is another critical component of crisis resilience. Many financially successful people are asset-rich but cash-poor, leaving them vulnerable during disruptions. AI continuously evaluates liquidity needs and ensures that access to capital exists when required. It balances long-term growth with short-term stability, preventing forced decisions during emergencies.

AI also helps individuals distinguish between temporary disruption and permanent change. Humans tend to overreact to short-term pain and underreact to long-term trends. AI corrects this imbalance. It identifies whether a crisis requires immediate structural changes or simple patience. This prevents irreversible mistakes made under stress.

Tax strategy during uncertainty becomes even more important. Crises often create unique tax opportunities, such as lower income years ideal for Roth conversions or asset repositioning. AI identifies these windows and acts decisively. What feels like a setback can become a long-term advantage when viewed through an intelligent system. Ultimately, AI transforms uncertainty from a threat into a variable. It does not promise immunity from hardship. It promises preparedness. When uncertainty arrives—and it always does—AI ensures that clarity remains.

The Year the Ground Moved Beneath Olivia

Olivia had always believed she was prepared. She had saved consistently, avoided excessive debt, and made thoughtful financial decisions. Her life was stable, predictable, and carefully planned. Then, within the span of six months, everything she relied on began to shift.

The company Olivia had worked for over a decade announced restructuring. Her role was eliminated with little warning. At the same time, her father's health declined rapidly, requiring both emotional and financial support. Markets were volatile, news was bleak, and the future felt suddenly fragile. For the first time in her adult life, Olivia felt financially exposed—not because she had done something wrong, but because life had changed faster than her plans could adapt.

At first, panic whispered quietly. She considered selling investments to feel safer. She delayed decisions, hoping clarity would return on its own. Nights grew restless as questions piled up. How long would her savings last? Should she take the first job offered, even if it meant sacrificing long-term goals? Would helping her family compromise her own future?

It was during one of those restless nights that Olivia turned to the AI financial system she had set up months earlier but rarely needed. With trembling hands, she updated her income status and noted the changes in her expenses. She braced herself for bad news. What she received instead was calm.

The system did not react emotionally. It recalculated. It showed Olivia multiple paths forward, each with clear implications. One scenario assumed extended unemployment. Another modeled part-time income. Another explored a career pivot she had quietly dreamed about but never believed was possible. None of the paths were catastrophic. Some were uncomfortable. Some were surprisingly hopeful.

The AI highlighted something Olivia had overlooked: her liquidity was stronger than she realized. She had more flexibility than fear allowed her to see. It showed her that selling investments immediately would create unnecessary losses, while patience would preserve long-term stability. It identified tax opportunities created by her temporary lower income—opportunities that could strengthen her future rather than weaken it.

As weeks passed, Olivia began to trust the process. She accepted temporary work aligned with her skills rather than rushing into fear-driven decisions. She supported her father without guilt, knowing the impact was manageable. When markets dipped further, she did not panic. The system had already modeled the outcome.

Months later, Olivia found herself in a new role—different from her old job, but more aligned with her life. Her income stabilized. Her father's health improved. The crisis slowly receded. When Olivia reviewed her financial dashboard, she was surprised by what she saw. Her net worth had not collapsed. In some areas, it had improved.

More importantly, something inside Olivia had changed. The crisis had not broken her confidence. It had strengthened it. She had learned that preparedness was not about preventing disruption, but about responding intelligently when it arrived.

Years later, Olivia would reflect on that year as a turning point. Not because everything went wrong, but because she learned how to remain steady when it did. The AI had not removed uncertainty from her life. It had removed fear from her decisions.

In that year when the ground moved beneath her, Olivia discovered that clarity was not the absence of chaos. It was the presence of a system that could stand within it.

And from that moment forward, uncertainty no longer felt like an enemy. It felt like a challenge she knew how to meet.

Chapter 9

How AI Prepares You for the Financial Future Before It Arrives

The future has always been the most dangerous place for financial plans. Not because it is unknowable, but because it is misunderstood. Most people plan as if tomorrow will look like today, with minor variations. Artificial intelligence rejects this assumption entirely. It treats the future as a shifting landscape of probabilities rather than a single destination. By doing so, AI allows individuals to prepare for change long before it arrives, transforming uncertainty into strategic advantage.

Traditional financial planning relies heavily on linear projections. Income grows at a steady rate. Markets return an average number. Expenses follow predictable paths. Real life rarely behaves this way. AI replaces linear thinking with probabilistic modeling. It simulates thousands of potential futures, accounting for changes in tax laws, economic cycles, technological disruption, longevity, healthcare costs, and lifestyle shifts. This approach does not attempt to predict exactly what will happen. It prepares you for what could happen. One of the most powerful capabilities of AI is early detection. Financial risk often appears subtly before becoming obvious. A growing tax burden, declining purchasing power, or excessive concentration in one asset can quietly undermine long-term stability. AI identifies these trends early, when adjustments are small and painless rather than urgent and costly. This proactive awareness allows individuals to stay ahead of problems instead of reacting to them.

Opportunity detection is equally important. The future is not only a source of risk. It is a source of leverage. AI identifies windows of opportunity created by changes in income, market conditions, or tax law. These moments are often brief and easily missed. By monitoring continuously, AI ensures that opportunities are recognized and acted upon at the optimal time.

Technological change itself is a major driver of future financial disruption. Careers evolve, industries disappear, and new income streams emerge. AI integrates these possibilities into financial planning by modeling income volatility, retraining periods, and alternative revenue paths. This ensures that financial strategies remain resilient even as work and income structures change.

Longevity is another critical variable. Advances in healthcare and lifestyle may extend lifespans significantly, increasing the importance of long-term planning. AI models extended lifespans and adjusts income strategies accordingly. It ensures that wealth is not only sufficient for retirement, but for a long life that may include new phases of purpose, contribution, and growth.

Ultimately, preparing for the future is not about certainty. It is about readiness. AI creates readiness by transforming the unknown into something navigable. It allows individuals to move forward with confidence, knowing that whatever the future brings, their financial system is prepared to adapt.

The Future That Arrived Quietly for Jonathan

Jonathan had always thought of the future as something distant and abstract. He planned carefully, saved consistently, and followed conventional advice. He assumed that if he did everything "right," the future would take care of itself. For years, that belief seemed justified. His career progressed, his investments grew, and his life followed a familiar rhythm.

Then, gradually, the world around him began to change.

Jonathan's industry evolved faster than he expected. New technologies reshaped workflows. Younger professionals adapted quickly, while long-established roles began to fade. At first, Jonathan dismissed the changes as temporary. He had experience, stability, and a solid financial plan. He believed those would protect him.

But uncertainty crept in quietly. Opportunities narrowed. Expectations shifted. Jonathan realized that the future he had planned for was no longer the future forming around him. It was not a crisis yet—but it was no longer comfortable.

Around this time, Jonathan decided to adopt an AI-driven financial planning system. His motivation was not fear, but curiosity. He wanted to understand how prepared he truly was for what lay ahead. When he connected his financial life to the system, he expected confirmation that everything was on track. What he received instead was insight.

The AI did not alarm him. It simply showed him possibilities. It modeled scenarios where his income plateaued, declined, or shifted into new forms. It showed how his investments would perform under different economic conditions. It illustrated how changes in tax policy or healthcare costs could reshape his later years. None of the outcomes were disastrous—but some required adaptation.

For the first time, Jonathan saw the future not as a single path, but as a range of landscapes. Some were familiar. Others were unfamiliar but manageable. What mattered was not which future arrived, but whether he was prepared for all of them.

Over the next few years, Jonathan made gradual changes. He diversified income streams. He adjusted tax strategies. He invested in skills that aligned with emerging opportunities. None of these moves felt dramatic. They felt intentional. The AI guided each decision, showing long-term implications without urgency or fear.

Then one day, Jonathan noticed something remarkable. The future he had once worried about had arrived—but it did not feel threatening. His income had shifted, but not collapsed. His lifestyle had changed, but not diminished. His financial system adapted quietly, absorbing changes that would have once caused panic.

As time passed, Jonathan realized that the biggest transformation was internal. He no longer feared the unknown. He trusted his ability to adapt because his financial system was designed to do so. When new opportunities emerged, he could pursue them without risking stability. When challenges appeared, he could respond without desperation.

Years later, Jonathan reflected on how subtly everything had changed. There was no dramatic turning point, no single crisis that forced action. The future had arrived quietly, shaped by countless small adjustments guided by intelligent preparation.

Jonathan understood then that the purpose of planning was not to predict the future, but to remain capable within it. AI had not shown him exactly what would happen. It had ensured that whatever happened, he would not be unprepared.

In that quiet readiness, Jonathan found confidence. Not confidence in outcomes, but confidence in process. And with that confidence, the future no longer felt like something to fear—it felt like something he was ready to meet.

Chapter 10

The New Standard: Living a Fully Optimized Financial Life With AI

At the end of every technological shift, a new standard quietly replaces the old one. What once felt optional becomes expected. What once felt advanced becomes normal. Artificial intelligence is doing this to personal finance. The question is no longer whether AI can help with taxes, planning, or wealth protection. The question is how anyone manages complexity without it. This chapter is not about tools or tactics alone. It is about a new way of living with money.

For generations, financial planning was reactive. People responded to tax bills, market crashes, job changes, and retirement deadlines as they appeared. This approach was not a failure of discipline or intelligence. It was a failure of systems. Humans simply cannot process the number of variables required to manage a modern financial life optimally. AI changes that reality by making continuous optimization possible for individuals, not just institutions.

A fully optimized financial life does not mean perfection. It means alignment. Alignment between income and goals. Between taxes and strategy. Between risk and comfort.

Between present needs and future security. AI enables this alignment by integrating every part of your financial life into a single adaptive framework. Decisions no longer exist in isolation. Each action is evaluated in context, reducing unintended consequences.

This new standard also changes how people relate to money emotionally. Anxiety fades when uncertainty is replaced by understanding. Guilt disappears when spending aligns with strategy. Confidence grows when choices are backed by clear outcomes. AI does not remove responsibility. It enhances it by giving individuals the clarity needed to act wisely.

One of the most profound shifts AI introduces is time efficiency. Financial management no longer requires constant attention. Monitoring, recalibration, and optimization happen quietly in the background. This frees mental energy for creativity, relationships, and purpose. Money becomes a support system rather than a constant concern.

AI also democratizes financial intelligence. Strategies once reserved for the wealthy—tax arbitrage, asset location, withdrawal sequencing, generational planning—are now accessible to anyone willing to engage with intelligent systems. This closes the gap between financial knowledge and financial outcomes. The fully optimized financial life is not about chasing maximum wealth at all costs. It is about designing a system that supports the life you want to live. AI gives you the ability to define success on your own terms and build a financial structure that adapts as those terms evolve.

As this book concludes, one truth becomes clear: the future of personal finance is not manual, reactive, or fragmented. It is intelligent, adaptive, and human-centered. AI is not replacing financial wisdom. It is making it usable at scale. Those who embrace this shift will not only keep more of what they earn. They will live with greater freedom, clarity, and peace.

The Life That Finally Felt Complete

For most of his life, Thomas believed that financial stability was something you reached and then defended. He worked, saved, invested, and worried—always worried. Even in good years, he braced for setbacks. Even during calm periods, he anticipated disruption. Money had always felt like something that demanded vigilance, as if relaxing for too long would invite disaster.

Thomas's life was full. A career he respected. A family he loved. Yet beneath the surface, money occupied more space than he cared to admit. It shaped decisions quietly, sometimes subtly, sometimes loudly. Where he lived. How he worked.

When he rested. He told himself this was normal, that everyone lived this way.

Everything changed gradually, almost imperceptibly, after Thomas integrated AI into his financial life. At first, it was simply a convenience. Faster organization. Clearer projections. Better tax efficiency. But over time, something deeper began to shift.

The system did not demand attention. It did not flood him with alerts or decisions. It observed, learned, and adjusted. It anticipated tax changes before Thomas heard about them. It balanced risk without drama. It prepared for events Thomas had not yet imagined. And slowly, Thomas stopped worrying—not because he stopped caring, but because caring no longer required anxiety.

Years passed. His career evolved. His children grew and left home. His priorities shifted. Through every transition, the system adapted seamlessly. Income changed. Expenses transformed. Time horizons shortened. Nothing broke. Nothing panicked. His finances flowed with his life instead of resisting it.

As Thomas approached retirement, friends spoke nervously about the unknown. Would their money last? Would taxes explode? Would markets collapse at the worst possible time?

Thomas listened, empathetic but calm. He had seen these scenarios already—not as fears, but as modeled outcomes. He knew how his system would respond.

Retirement arrived quietly. There was no dramatic moment, no sharp dividing line. Work faded into choice rather than obligation. Income shifted smoothly. Taxes remained predictable. Markets moved, but Thomas's life did not shake with them. His days filled with meaning rather than maintenance.

One afternoon, years into retirement, Thomas sat alone in the same chair where he once obsessed over spreadsheets and projections. He realized that he had not thought about money anxiously in a very long time. Not because he was wealthy beyond measure, but because his financial life was complete. It worked. It supported him. It adapted without demanding his constant involvement.

Thomas reflected on how much energy he had spent worrying in the past—energy he could never recover. Yet he did not regret the journey. It had led him here, to a place where money no longer dictated his emotional state. Where planning had become presence. Where the future felt navigable rather than threatening.

He understood now that optimization was never about squeezing out every possible dollar. It was about removing friction between life and resources. It was about building a system strong enough to carry uncertainty without fear.

As the sun dipped low and the room grew quiet, Thomas smiled—not because everything was perfect, but because everything was aligned. His finances were no longer a project. They were a foundation.

And on that foundation, Thomas lived freely.

That was the true promise of AI-powered personal finance—not just better numbers, but a better life.

Final Thoughts

Financial freedom has never been about reaching a single number. It has always been about reaching a state of confidence—confidence that your decisions are sound, your future is supported, and your life is not vulnerable to avoidable mistakes. Throughout this book, one truth has surfaced repeatedly: money becomes powerful only when it is coordinated. Artificial intelligence is not changing finance because it is fast or advanced. It is changing finance because it finally makes coordination possible for individuals.

For decades, people were forced to manage their finances in fragments. Taxes were handled separately from investments. Retirement planning existed apart from income strategy. Estate planning was delayed, misunderstood, or ignored entirely. Each area worked independently, creating inefficiencies that quietly drained wealth year after year. AI brings these fragments together into a single, adaptive system that understands not just numbers, but consequences.

The most important shift AI introduces is perspective. Instead of reacting to financial events after they occur, AI allows individuals to anticipate outcomes before decisions are made. This transforms planning from a defensive activity into a proactive one. Taxes stop being surprises. Market volatility stops being paralyzing. Retirement stops being uncertain. Wealth stops being fragile.

This book has shown that AI does not replace responsibility—it enhances it. It gives individuals the ability to see clearly, choose intentionally, and adapt continuously. It removes emotional extremes from financial decision-making and replaces them with clarity. Fear loses its power when outcomes are understood. Overconfidence fades when risks are modeled honestly. Balance becomes possible.

Another truth revealed through this journey is that optimization is not about perfection. Life is unpredictable, and no system can remove uncertainty entirely. What AI does is make uncertainty navigable. It ensures that no single event—whether economic, personal, or political—has the power to derail an entire financial life. It builds resilience rather than rigidity.

Perhaps the most profound outcome of AI-powered financial planning is peace. Peace that comes from knowing nothing important is being ignored. Peace that comes from seeing the full picture rather than guessing. Peace that allows people to focus on living rather than managing money constantly. When finances run intelligently in the background, life moves to the foreground.

This book is not a prediction of the future. It is a reflection of the present. AI is already reshaping how people earn, invest, plan, and protect wealth. Those who adopt intelligent systems early gain not just financial advantages, but emotional ones. They gain time, clarity, and freedom.

As you close this book, remember this: wealth is not built in moments of intensity. It is built through systems that work quietly over time. Artificial intelligence is the most powerful financial system individuals have ever had access to—not because it promises more money, but because it protects what matters.

The future of personal finance will not belong to those who work harder, worry more, or react faster. It will belong to those who build intelligent systems and allow those systems to evolve with them.

Your financial life does not need to be perfect. It needs to be aligned. AI makes that alignment possible.

www.ingramcontent.com/pod-product-compliance
Lightning Source LLC
LaVergne TN
LVHW022027200926
848481LV00007B/2570